*The* WHALE-
WATCHER'S
HANDBOOK

D1018817

# The WHALE-WATCHER'S HANDBOOK

## A Field Guide to the Whales, Dolphins, and Porpoises of North America

▲

## DAVID K. BULLOCH

*Illustrations by Lou Burlingame*

LYONS & BURFORD

Design by Judy Morgan

Printed in the United States of America

10 9 8 7 6 5 4 3 2 1

Library of Congress Cataloging-in-Publication Data

Bulloch, David K.
    The whalewatcher's handbook: a guide to the whales, dolphins, and porpoises of North America/by David K. Bulloch: illustrated by Lou Burlingame.
        p.        cm.
    "An American Littoral Society book."
    Includes bibliographical references (p. 111).
    ISBN 1-55821-232-9
    1.  Whale watching—North America—Guidebooks.      2.  Cetacea—North America.  I.  Title.
QL737.C4B864   1993
599.5'097—dc20
                                                                    93-7113
                                                                        CIP

# ACKNOWLEDGMENTS

The major sources of information for this book include two National Oceanic and Atmospheric Administration Technical Reports: NMFS Circ–396, "Whales, Dolphins, and Porpoises of the Western North Atlantic," by Stephen Leatherwood, David K. Caldwell, and Howard Winn; and NMFS Circ–444, "Whales, Dolphins, and Porpoises of the Eastern North Pacific and Adjacent Arctic Waters," by Stephen Leatherwood, Randall Reeves, William Perrin, and William Evans. Both volumes are out of print. We have made use of many of their photographs as well as a few of their line drawings.

Claire Steimle and Judy Berrien of the National Marine Fisheries Service library at Sandy Hook, New Jersey, helped me dig out much pertinent literature.

Derek Bennett, executive director of the American Littoral Society, made this project possible and offered helpful suggestions during its gestation.

Lou Burlingame drew the graceful illustrations that appear in every profile and on the cover, and supplied the photos of the Humpback diving sequence.

Over the years, I have talked to many whalewatchers who gave me ideas on points of identification and alerted me to the identification problems many species present. I cannot credit all by name but can at least collectively thank them for sharing their insights with me.

—David K. Bulloch
January, 1993

# CONTENTS

# ABOUT THE AMERICAN LITTORAL SOCIETY

The American Littoral Society is a non-profit organization whose members share a fascination with the life of the sea. Their special interests are with those animals, plants, and habitats close to shore in the coastal ocean, estuaries, salt-water wetlands, tidal flats, and coral reefs.

The Society has published its own "Special Publications" and has supported the publication of other books that further its twin goals of marine conservation and public education. These publications include "The Wasted Ocean," which covers the history, extent, damage, and cures for marine pollution, and "Underwater Naturalist," which looks at common animal life below the tidelines of the United States coastline.

The Society publishes a quarterly, the "Underwater Naturalist," as well as regional and national newsletters concerning member activities and coastal issues.

The Society conducts field trips ranging in length from one day to one week. These have included natural history-oriented sojourns to Maine, South Florida, Bermuda, the Bahamas, Belize, and a great many other locations.

The Society also runs seminars and workshops, some of general interest, and others on specialized topics such as non-point source pollution.

The Society conducts the world's largest volunteer fish tag-and-release program. Members tag about ten thousand fish annually. Tag returns from recaptured fish help scientists determine migration patterns.

To find out more about the Society and what you can do to improve the marine environment and extend your knowledge of the marine world, write: American Littoral Society, Sandy Hook, Highlands, NJ 07732, or call (908) 291-0055.

# PREFACE

For the marine naturalist, whalewatching provides another reason to go to sea and visit new shores. Since both are deliberate acts, you will probably ask yourself, "How will I know what I will see and how will I recognize it?" Hence the need for this guide.

This guide is limited to the whales, dolphins, and porpoises of North American waters. There is not much sense in describing a Tasman Beaked Whale or an Irrawaddy Dolphin, unless you plan to venture halfway around the world to see them.

There is also little sense in enumerating creatures that appear to occur in North American waters, but are so elusive or rare that they are almost never seen at sea or, if seen, are nearly impossible to identify at a distance. These are mainly the Beaked Whales. Some are known only from a few washed-up carcasses. Most require close examination of the teeth in the jaw to identify them positively.

By limiting geographic coverage and removing rare and seldom seen cetaceans from a worldwide list of seventy-six species, we can reduce the list of possible sightings to a more manageable size. However, this does not mean that identifying those on the "short list" will be easy. Whales lie low in the water and, with a sea running, are not easy to view. Dolphins swim rapidly, and small groups spend more time beneath the waves than exposed at the surface. Given choppy water or poor lighting (if the light is behind the critter, it will appear black no matter how well marked it may be), or difficulty closing in for a better look, you may not be able to come up with a positive identification.

Although stray individuals or small pods may show up almost anywhere at any time of year, whales, dolphins, and porpoises have favorite swimming grounds at certain times of the year. Knowing this will help you plan your trip and alert you to special viewing locations. A section has been provided that describes the likeliest places certain species are apt to be found and the best time of year to see them. Even so, check with the local references given (see Appendix 1) to be sure the whales have arrived. Whales are as subject to contingencies as humans and, to some extent, are "where you find 'em."

# ABOUT WHALES

Whales, dolphins, and porpoises are air-breathing mammals that maintain a steady body temperature, bear live young and nurse them, and are especially adapted for living their entire lives in water. Their noses, one or two blowholes, are on the top of their heads, their arms are now flippers, and their legs have disappeared and been replaced with tail flukes.

Taxonomically, these mammals belong to the order Cetacea which, in turn, consists of two suborders: the Mysticeti, the Baleen or Whalebone Whales, whose teeth have been replaced by plates that act as strainers while feeding; and Odontoceti, the toothed whales, dolphins, and porpoises, whose mouths bear true teeth.

There are nine species of Baleen Whales (all but the Bowhead are covered here) that are grouped into three families, Rorquals, Right, and Gray Whales. All Baleen Whales have paired blowholes. Beneath their lower jaw, extending rearward to their flippers, they have pleated throat grooves, which can unfold and enormously increase the amount of water they can scoop up prior to filtering for food. Popular whale literature portrays Baleen Whales eating plankton, implying that they subsist by filtering out microscopic organisms. In reality, Baleen Whales seldom feed on anything less than one or two inches long and things that are present in great quantities, such as shrimplike krill, squid, and small fish.

The toothed whales have a single blowhole and anywhere from twenty to two hundred and fifty teeth, most of which erupt through the gums. The Beaked Whales and the Narwhal are among the exceptions. Of the thirty-nine species of toothed whales that have been reported to occur in North American waters, only twenty are treated in this guide. Those omitted are pelagic (usually living in open sea), cryptic, and elusive, or otherwise rare. You may get to see one or two of the species not covered here, but it will likely be a carcass washed up on a beach. A complete list of whales, dolphins, and porpoises occurring in North American waters is given in Appendix 2.

Because of the different anatomy of their mouths, Baleen and toothed whales have different diets. Baleen whales take in food either by gulping or skimming, straining out smaller creatures that normally occur in large pods—shrimp-like crustaceans, squid, and small fish, for example. Toothed whales may also feed on shrimp, squid, and fishes, but will also eat larger prey. For example, the Sperm Whale will eat giant squid and the Killer Whale often hunts seals and whales of other species.

The taxonomic separation of whales, dolphins, and porpoises into species is, among some, still problematic. Is the Cochito truly a separate species or a race of Harbor Porpoise? In captivity, the Bottlenose Dolphin has bred with the Rough-

1

toothed Dolphin, Risso's Dolphin, and others. The offspring have not lived long enough to indicate whether they can breed, but the Bottlenose-Risso's Dolphin hybrid has been seen alive and well in the wild. So have hybrids of the Dusky Dolphin and the Pacific White-sided Dolphin, as well as hybrids among Baleen Whales.

A few words about the terminology used in describing a whale or dolphin's external features may be helpful. The top or back of the animal is the dorsal side. The underside or belly is the ventral side. Along the dorsal mid-line, which roughly corresponds to the centerline of the head and the top of the spinal column, you will find such prominent features as head ridges, blowhole(s), splash

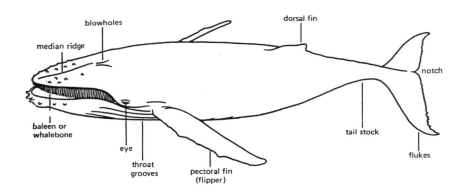

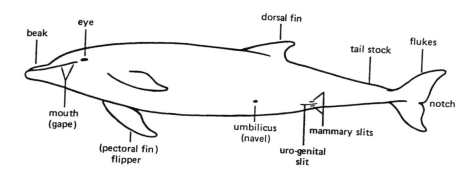

guards around blowholes, a dorsal fin or hump, and ridges or bumps extending down the tail stock. The dorsal fin varies considerably in size and shape between species and, to a lesser extent, within species, usually according to age or sex. Thus the dorsal fin in a mature male Killer Whale is a high triangular sail, while in the young and among the females, it is smaller and more falcate. If the dorsal fin is recurved, that is, if the trailing edge is concave, it is said to be falcate. The recurvature can be severe (extremely falcate) or barely noticeable. The tip of the dorsal fin may be pointed or rounded, often a useful diagnostic feature.

The pectoral fins or flippers vary in length, breadth, and shape, and can range from stubby paddles to long sicklelike appendages. They can also vary from smooth-edged to ragged, bumpy surfaces.

The tail or flukes vary among and within species. They may have a very distinct center notch to no notch at all. Their trailing edge can be mildly concave, convex, or square, and either smooth or ragged. Individuals of certain species (Humpback Whales, for example) have individual shade patterns on the underside of the flukes, as well as distinctive indentations that are usually the result of the wear and tear of living.

On the ventral side, a few whales have a ventral keel, a ridge superimposed on the normal taper of the tail stock. Up forward, on Baleen Whales, throat grooves or pleats extend from the mouth to just under the flippers. These unfold when the whale gulps up water prior to sieving out food.

Head shape variations are important in identifying species, but the distinctions between some whales and dolphins are not as easy to describe as they are to discern visually. A melon is a forehead swelling, and a callosity or bonnet is a rounded, disklike protuberance. In Baleen Whales, raised regions around the blowholes are called splash guards.

The natural history and behavior of a number of species of whales, dolphins, and porpoises are all but unknown. For other species that congregate in the same waters year after year and follow predictable migration routes, a great deal is known, right down to individual recognition and family ties. The Humpback, Killer, and Gray Whales have made good subjects for such studies.

If you want to know more about whales, the literature is enormous and popular books abound. Less well known is the ever-growing body of scientific literature. If you develop a curiosity about a particular species—their migration patterns, family groups, sounds, and communication patterns—you can assuage it by inquiring into that literature or taking a few whale study courses given by various institutions in the United States and Canada. A list of places that might help is given in Appendix 3.

# LARGE WHALES
## (over 40 feet)

# BLUE WHALE
### *(Balaenoptera musculus)*

**Description:** Maximum length 85 feet. The largest living mammal. A Baleen Whale. Broad U-shaped head with prominent splash guards around the blowholes. Small dorsal fin, only a foot high, variable in shape, placed well aft, about three-quarters of its body length, that is seldom visible except as it begins a dive.

It has broad flukes, as wide as one-quarter of its body length. Their trailing edge is usually straight or slightly concave. Their flippers are long and pointed.

The body is bluish gray with light gray mottling. The underside of the body is light, often yellowish or a mustard color. The undersides of the flippers are white. The baleen is black.

Its blow averages 30 feet in height and is slender and vertical.

**Variability:** The dorsal fin shape ranges from triangular and pointed to falcate and rounded.

**Range:** In the western North Atlantic, in spring and summer, they are found as far north as the Arctic Circle. They appear on the Nova Scotian banks, the St. Lawrence Gulf and estuary, and the Grand Banks. Tend to be pelagic when migrating but have been seen close to shore.

North Pacific movement patterns are not well known. Usually sighted far offshore. They are spotted regularly between February and April at the mouth of the Gulf of California, also occasionally in the fall, but not between November and January. Can be seen along the California coast between July and October, usually outside the Channel Islands.

**Behavior:** Normally travels alone or in pairs.

Their blow is tall, to 30 feet, and straight. If moving slowly, the blowholes and head will be visible and the dorsal fin may break the surface. Moving quickly, or when about to dive, the head and blowholes submerge, the dorsal fin appears, and the flukes rise slightly above the surface before going below. Dives average 10 to

huge, to 85 feet

U–shaped head

bluish body

baleen all black

blow is 30 feet high

raises flukes when diving

compare with Fin Whale

20 minutes. When surfaced, it will blow 8 to 15 times, making shallow dives of 12- to 15-second duration between blows, before sounding.

**Lookalikes:** Difficult to distinguish from a Fin Whale at a distance. Closer up, its mottled blue-gray color is clearly different from the gray of a Fin, which also has a white lower lip that is easy to see. Its baleen is all black, whereas a Fin is a bluish gray with yellowish white stripes. Its head is broader than a Fin. A Fin has a higher dorsal fin.

*Top*. Note the U-shaped head, the tall blow, and the raised splash guards forward of the blow holes.

*Bottom through p.11 top*. Dive sequence of a fast-swimming blue whale.

*Below*. Although the flukes are raised high here, they often barely break water during the dive.

# FIN WHALE
*(Balaenoptera physalus)*

**Description:** Maximum length 79 feet. A Baleen Whale. Its head is flattened and V–shaped with a prominent ridge and raised splash guard forward of its blowholes. Its dorsal fin can be up to two feet tall, falcate, with a rounded tip, and set back more than two-thirds of its body length. The dorsal fin is exposed shortly after the whale blows.

There is a prominent ridge on the back behind the dorsal fin.

Back and sides are dark gray to brownish black. Skin is rarely mottled or heavily scarred. Just behind the head there is a white to gray chevron whose apex is on the mid-line and whose arms point rearward. The undersides, including flukes and flippers, are white. On the head, on the right side only, the lower lip is white that may extend up to the upper lip and neck in some individuals. The forward baleen plates on the right side are yellowish white. The rest, right and left, are striped with alternate bands of yellowish white and blue gray.

**Variability:** The white coloration above the lip varies in individuals, as does the shape and setback of the dorsal fin.

**Range:** Widely distributed in the Atlantic and Pacific. The most numerous of the big whales. In the western Atlantic, they summer from temperate waters to the Arctic Circle. In winter they range south into the Caribbean and Gulf of Mexico. Often seen close to shore in large numbers in the Gulf of Maine from March through June.

In the eastern North Pacific, in winter, they can be seen along the coast from Big Sur, California, to Cabo San Lucas, Baja California, and are especially common around the Channel Islands. In summer, they range north into the Gulf of Alaska and the Bering Sea.

12

**Behavior:** Fast swimmers to 20 knots. Travel alone, in pairs, or in small pods of 6 or 7, which sometimes merge into larger groups of 50 or so.

Its blow is 15 to 20 feet tall; an inverted cone or elliptical. When moving slowly, it exposes its dorsal fin shortly after blowing. When it surfaces from a deep dive, the top of the head usually breaks the surface first. After blowing, it arches its back, rolls forward, exposing its dorsal fin, and dives without exposing its flukes. It dives for 5 to 15 minutes (6 to 7 minutes is average), then blows for 3 to 7 times or more at regular intervals of several minutes, then dives again.

Fin Whales breach occasionally, reentering with a splash.

**Lookalikes:** Can be confused with the Blue Whale, the Sei Whale, and in southern waters, with Bryde's Whale. Bryde's Whale has three ridges on its head and has a smaller, more pointed dorsal fin. The Blue Whale is bluish gray and mottled, its head is broad and U-shaped, its baleen is all black, and its dorsal fin is smaller and often triangular.

The dorsal fin of a Sei Whale is sharply pointed and set farther forward than on the Fin. As it surfaces, its head and dorsal fin surface almost simultaneously. Its blow is smaller (10 to 15 feet). As it dives, it doesn't arch its back as much. On the surface, it blows at regular intervals for long periods of time.

*Top.* Note the long, tapering head and the sharp, well-defined ridge which gave it the nickname "razorback".

The sharp ridge and the asymmetric white lip (white on the right side only) are good field keys to the Fin.

# SEI WHALE
*(Balaenoptera borealis)*

**Description:** Maximum length 62 feet. A Baleen Whale. Its head is not as V-shaped as the Fin nor as U-shaped as the Blue Whale. The splash guard in front of the blowholes is low, much less prominent than in the Fin or Blue Whale.

It has a single prominent ridge along the head to the blowhole. Its blow is similar to the Fin but not as high (10 to 15 feet). Its dorsal fin varies in height from 10 to 22 inches, is highly falcate, and is set forward more than a third the distance from the tail to the tip of the head, much more so than the Fin or the Blue.

Its back, sides, and rear underside are dark bluish gray. Its flippers and flukes are dark, as is the lower lip and mouth cavity. Its body has a galvanized appearance from gray-white scarring. Its baleen is uniformly grayish black. Some have a few light plates forward.

**Variability:** Size of the dorsal fin varies, as does the color of the forward baleen plates.

**Range:** Pelagic, temperate water species found in both the Atlantic and Pacific. Its range is poorly known. It migrates northward along the northeast United States and Canadian coasts in June and July, and can be seen off eastern Newfoundland in August and September. It is abundant in Placentia Bay, Newfoundland, in August.

It is sparsely distributed from the central California coast south to Baja California in winter. In summer, it can be found west of the Channel Islands to as far north as the Gulf of Alaska. Common off central California in late summer and early fall.

**Behavior:** Alone or in groups of 2 to 5 individuals. Fast swimmers, over 20 knots. They feed by skimming near the surface and are not deep divers. They surface at a shallow angle, thus the blowhole and dorsal fin appear simultaneously. They usually remain visible for long periods. As they dive, they seldom arch their backs high or expose their flukes. Because they feed just below the surface, their flukes may leave swirl patterns. They blow at regular intervals on the surface.

**Lookalikes:** At a distance, it is very hard to distinguish a Sei from a Fin or Bryde's Whale. Closer up, the white color of the lower lip separates the Fin and, closer still, the single head ridge of the Sei and the three ridges of Bryde's Whale distinguishes those two.

It has also been confused with the Blue Whale, but its smaller size and its relatively larger dorsal fin set farther forward on its back help tell them apart.

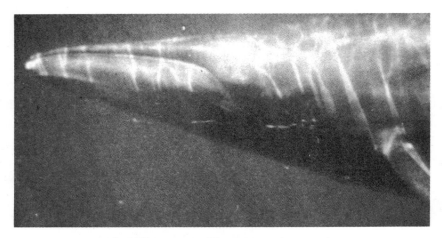

*Above*. Note the prominent falcate (recurved) dorsal fin.

*Left*. Underwater views of the Sei (pronounced "say") whale. The dappled and streaked appearance is due to surface reflection, not skin pigmentation.

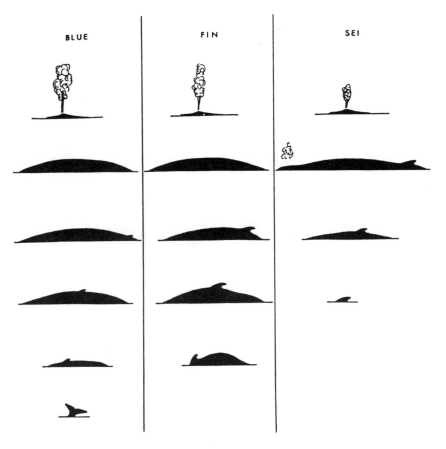

Profile characteristics of the Blue, Fin, and Sei Whales: blowing, surfacing, and diving

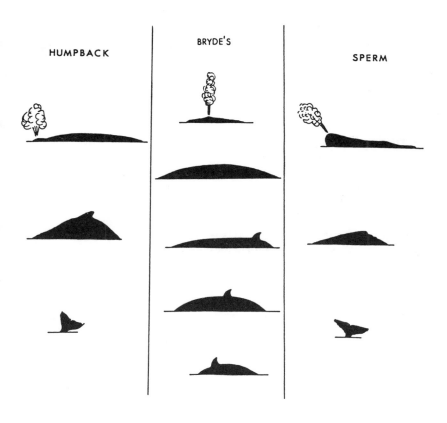

Profile characteristics of the Humpback, Bryde's, and Sperm Whales: blowing, surfacing, and diving

# BRYDE'S WHALE
## *(Balaenoptera edeni)*

**Description:** Maximum length 46 feet. A Baleen Whale. Closely resembles the Sei Whale in profile and general appearance.

It has three ridges forward of its blowhole, although the outer two may not be as high or as distinct as the central ridge in some individuals. The dorsal fin can be nearly two feet high, is extremely falcate, pointed at its tip, and located about a third of the way forward of the tail. Its trailing edge is often frayed or notched.

The body is smoky gray and smoothly colored. Some individuals have a light gray region on both sides just forward of the dorsal fin. The baleen is slate gray.

**Variability:** The prominence of the head ridges is variable. So is the height of the dorsal fin and the light coloration below the dorsal fin.

**Range:** Found worldwide in warm temperate waters. Has been reported from Virginia south into the Caribbean and the Gulf of Mexico. Rarely seen along the coast of California but common around the mouth of the Gulf of California.

**Behavior:** Usually single or in pairs. Up to 7 have been reported together. It surfaces steeply, like the Fin Whale, and blows well before exposing its dorsal fin. However, this varies and is not entirely reliable as a diagnostic. They occasionally breach. While swimming underwater they frequently change course. Sometimes they will approach a boat.

**Lookalikes:** Only an expert can separate a Bryde's Whale from a Sei at a distance. Close up, the three head ridges are distinctive. Also can be confused with the Fin, which can be quickly identified by its white right lower lip, and with the Minke, which has a much more angular head, a single head ridge, a single white band on each flipper, and is smaller (30 feet).

## FIELD MARKS:

large, to 46 feet
...............

Three ridges forward of
blowhole
...............

falcate dorsal fin
...............

compare with Sei and Minke
...............

*Top photo*. Note the distinct ridges forward of the blowholes and the falcate dorsal fin.

# HUMPBACK WHALE
## (Megaptera novaeangliae)

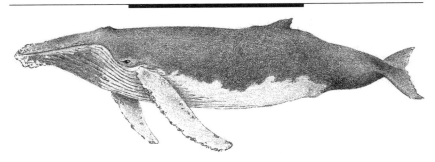

**Description:** Maximum length 53 feet. A Baleen Whale. Robust body with a broad, U-shaped head that has a series of knobs on top and on its lips. Its flippers are very long, one-third its body length, and scalloped on their leading edge. Its body narrows considerably behind its dorsal fin, which is set back somewhat more than two-thirds its body length. The dorsal fin is small and variable in shape, and appears to sit on a hump on its back.

Body color is black with a white belly, as are the undersides of flippers and flukes. Its body tends to be heavily encrusted with barnacles and whale lice, giving it a spotty white appearance.

Its blow is short (less than 10 feet) and bushy.

**Variability:** The coloration of the undersides of the flukes and their notch marks help distinguish one individual from another via comparison photographs. The dorsal fin varies from a nubbin to a low, rounded, falcate fin.

**Range:** In the western North Atlantic, its migration routes take it from the Caribbean past Bermuda on to Stellwagen Bank, the Gulf of Maine, Newfoundland, Labrador, and beyond in spring.

In the eastern North Pacific, in summer it ranges from Pt. Conception to Prince William Sound, Alaska. One stock winters off Hawaiian waters from November to March. Another winters along the coast of Baja California, principally around Gorda Bank, into the Gulf of California.

**Behavior:** Humpbacks are gregarious, often in groups of 7 to 10 individuals. They are highly acrobatic, breaching repeatedly, slapping the water with flippers, flukes, and body. They often raise one flipper aloft.

The Humpback's blow is short, 10 feet or less, and balloon-shaped. Usually it blows 4 to 8 times between dives. As they dive, they arch their backs high and raise their flukes well clear of the water.

26

**Lookalikes:** From a distance, they can be confused with any of the larger whales. However, they arch their backs and raise their flukes high when diving (unless they are in shallow water), which separates them from all but the Sperm Whale. The flukes of the Sperm Whale are dark and even along their trailing edge, while the undersides of the Humpback's flukes are white and their edges are ragged.

## FIELD MARKS:

large, to 53 feet

knobs on head

small dorsal fin sits on hump

long ragged flippers, white underneath

short bushy blow

acrobatic

raises flukes when diving

compare with Blue Whale

Dive Sequence of the Humpback Whale.

# SPERM WHALE
*(Physeter macrocephalus/catadon)*

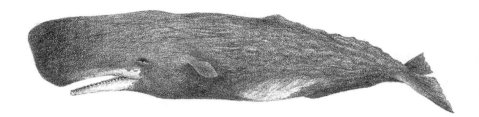

**Description:** Maximum length 50 feet. A toothed whale. Huge head, almost a third of its body length, is squared off, giving it a boxcar shape. It has a single blowhole set well forward on the head and set to the left of its midline. Its blow is small (8 feet), bushy, and at a sharp angle to the left. Its snout sits well over its jaws.

It has no dorsal fin but has a distinct rounded dorsal hump set back about two-thirds its body length. Behind the hump are a series of bumps along its midline. These can be clearly seen as the animal begins a dive. The whale also has a ventral keel that can be seen as it dives. Its flukes are broad and triangular with a deep notch.

The body is a dark brownish gray except for the belly and front of the head, which may be gray to off-white. The skin around the mouth is white. The skin behind the neck has a shriveled appearance.

**Variability:** The undersides of the flukes and flippers vary in color, mainly shades of brown and black.

**Range:** Widely distributed but northward in summer and in the lower latitudes in winter. They avoid polar ice. In the western North Atlantic, they migrate to the New England Grand Banks, Newfoundland, and Labrador coasts in August and September.

In the eastern North Pacific, they are relatively common over the continental slope of California and Baja California from November through April. In summer, they can be seen along the coast of British Columbia, especially around the Queen Charlotte Islands.

**Behavior:** Gregarious, in groups up to 50 individuals. Older males are solitary. Seldom seen in water less than 600 feet deep. They are deep divers and can spend over an hour below. Upon surfacing, they emit a loud blow and may remain on the

## FIELD MARKS:

large, to 50 feet

boxcar head

dorsal hump and bumpy spine

no dorsal fin

low blow (8 feet) and forward

raises flukes when diving

surface up to 10 minutes, repeatedly blowing before diving again. As they begin their dive, they throw their flukes high in the air. The young will occasionally breach.

**Lookalikes:** Because of the unusual shape of the head, they are not likely to be confused with any of the other large whales.

Sperm Whales usually show their flukes when starting a long, deep dive. Note the smooth trailing edges and triangular shapes of the flukes.

Profiles of the Sperm Whale at the surface and its diving sequence.

# RIGHT WHALE
*(Eubalaena glacialis)*

**Description:** Maximum length 53 feet. A Baleen Whale. Rotund body with a smooth dark back without a dorsal fin or dorsal ridge. Its upper jaw is long, nearly a fourth its body length, narrow, arched, and covered with bumps called callosities, the largest of which is called a bonnet that lies just in front of its blowholes. The callosities are usually covered with barnacles and whale-lice, which gives them a yellowish white hue. The two blowholes are widely separated.

Its back and sides are black or brownish black. Its chin and belly are white. The baleen plates are dark, although if the animal swims with its mouth open, the plates appear light. Baleen is missing in front and, head on, the opening is shaped like a pup tent.

**Variability:** Skin can have a mottled appearance.

**Range:** Widely distributed but sparse. In the western North Atlantic, they begin to move north along the eastern Florida coast between January and March, past New England in spring, and as far north as Nova Scotia and Labrador in summer. They have been seen in the Gulf of Mexico in winter.

Very sparse in the eastern North Pacific and only occasionally seen along the coasts of California, Oregon, and Washington.

**Behavior:** Travel singly or in pairs. Slow swimmers, not wary of boats.
As they dive, they throw their flukes clear of the water. They will occasionally leap clear of the water and land with a booming splash. Will often wave a flipper above the water.

Their blow is distinctly V-shaped, with two obvious bushy spouts.

**Lookalikes:** Not likely to be confused with any other large whale.

A Right Whale off the northeastern Florida coast. Mothers and calves appear in early spring on their annual migration northward. Note the lack of a dorsal fin.

Dive sequence and blow of the Right Whale

# GRAY WHALE
*(Eschrichtius robustus)*

**Description:** Maximum length 45 feet. A Baleen Whale. Body is tapered at both ends. The head is narrow and triangular. The mouth moderately arched and, from a side view, steeply sloped. Tip of the upper jaw usually protrudes over the lower jaw. The back has no dorsal fin but has a low hump about two-thirds back along its body, followed by a ridge of bumps along its mid-line.

It has broad flukes with a deep notch and small flippers with pointed tips.

Mottled gray skin, heavily encrusted with barnacles on the body, head, and tail. Orange whale-lice create orange patches among the white barnacles. Their baleen is short and yellowish white.

**Variability:** The young are uniformly dark and barnacle free.

**Range:** Pacific only. In winter, January through March, they concentrate in several areas along the outer coast of Baja California, Scammon's Lagoon, San Ignacio Lagoon, and Magdalena Bay. In the spring, they head northward close to shore except at the California Bight, where they pass westward of the Channel Islands. A few spend summer along the coast of British Columbia, but most head for the Bering Sea and points north. In the fall, they reverse their migration pattern southward.

**Behavior:** When migrating, they travel alone or in small groups rarely larger than 16 individuals. They are quite active. They breach occasionally during migration and regularly on their wintering grounds. They often spyhop and lobtail (raise their flukes and slam them on the water). Often quite unafraid of boats and will come alongside a small boat.

Their blow is low (10 feet or so), bushy, and either heart-shaped or V-shaped. They blow 3 to 5 times at intervals of 30 to 50 seconds, and submerge for 3 to 5 minutes. Their average swimming speed while migrating is 4 mph. When feeding, they stir up large clouds of mud.

large, to 45 feet

no dorsal fin

mottled and encrusted skin

bushy, heart-shaped blow

Pacific only

compare with Right and Sperm
Whale

**Lookalikes:** The absence of a dorsal fin might confuse the whale with a Sperm or Right Whale. The Right Whale has a conspicuous bonnet on its head and the Sperm Whale's head is squarish, not triangular, as is the Gray Whale's.

# BAIRD'S BEAKED WHALE
## (Berardius bairdii)

**Description:** Maximum length: 42 feet, male; 35 feet, female. Bulging forehead that slopes down to a long and cylindrical beak. Lower jaw protrudes beyond the upper jaw, exposing teeth that create the appearance of a white-tipped snout. Long, rotund body with a nearly triangular dorsal fin located well behind the middle of the body. The flukes have a straight trailing edge with little or no notch. Flippers are untapered and have rounded tips. Color ranges from brown to slate gray or black, with white patches on the underside of the throat between its flippers and on its navel. Body is often heavily scarred.

**Variability:** Dorsal fin tip may be more or less rounded and its rear margin from straight to mildly concave.

**Range:** In North Pacific, mainly offshore. Its southern limit is about 28 degrees north latitude off Baja California. To the north, it has been found stranded in the Bering Sea. Appears off central California coast in July and October, and has been seen off Washington between April and October. It has been encountered regularly off Vancouver Island, British Columbia, from May through September.

**Behavior:** Travels in pods from 2 to 30 animals that swim in tight formation and breathe synchronously while moving.

As the whale surfaces to breathe, its head often emerges at a steep angle, enough to see the long cylindrical beak and bulbous head. It surfaces in a wheellike motion that exposes its dorsal fin, which is set back nearly two-thirds the length of its body. The flukes are sometimes raised as it dives. Its blow is low and indistinct.

It rarely breaches. It's said to be difficult to approach but this is not always so.

**Lookalikes:** Can be initially confused with a Minke Whale but the Minke has a flat, triangular head, a more falcate dorsal fin that appears on the surface simultaneously with its blow, and a white band on each flipper.

When Baird's Beaked Whale lies on the surface, its dorsal fin does not emerge. That and its bulbous head can lead one to confuse it with a Sperm Whale, but the oblique blow of the Sperm Whale and its boxcar appearance will separate the two. If you see a whale nearly fitting this description in the Atlantic, it is probably the Northern Bottlenose Whale. Baird's Beaked Whale is found only on the Pacific side of the United States.

Aerial view of a herd of Baird's Beaked Whales. You can see the bulbous forehead and the long white-tipped beak.

The body of a Baird's Beaked Whale is commonly streaked with long scars that cover nearly the entire exposed surface. It is the largest of the beaked whales, all of which are either rare or won't approach boats.

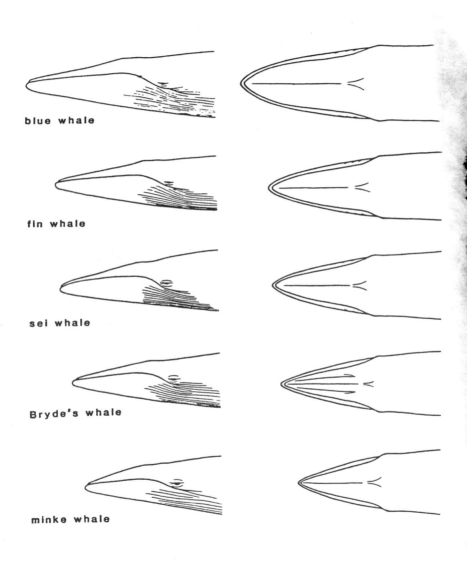

blue whale

fin whale

sei whale

Bryde's whale

minke whale

Side and underside views of the heads of the large common whales.

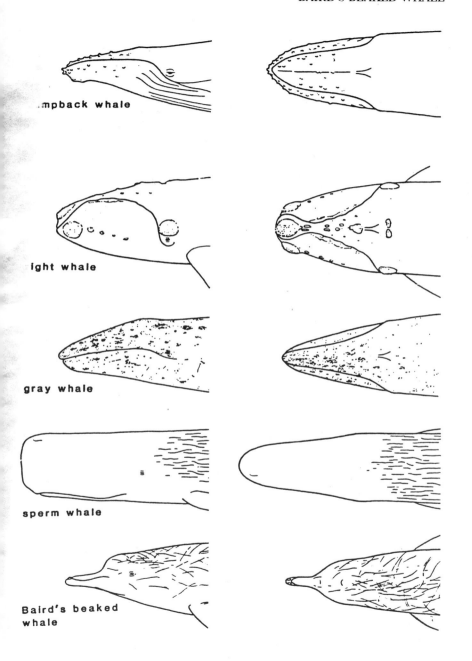

# MEDIUM WHALES
## (under 35 feet)

# MINKE WHALE
## *(Balaenoptera acutorostrata)*

**Description:** Maximum length (Northern Hemisphere): 26 feet, female; 23 feet, male. The smallest of the Baleen Whales. Flat, narrow, triangular head with a single ridge along the top. Sleek body shape.

Tall falcate dorsal fin located over two-thirds of the way back on the body. Its dorsal fin is visible simultaneously with its low, inconspicuous blow. Black to dark-gray back. The belly is white as are the undersides of the flippers. There is a white band on the upper surface of each flipper. Sometimes there is a wide, light chevron behind the head and a swath of light gray on its sides. Its baleen is yellowish white, although the posterior plates are brown to black.

**Variability:** Body coloration, especially light areas above and behind the flippers and just in front of and below the dorsal fin, varies among individual animals.

**Range:** In both the Atlantic and Pacific, from polar ice to equatorial waters. Most abundant in temperate waters in the Atlantic where they often approach close to shore and enter river mouths, inlets, and estuaries. They approach the Canadian coast in May and June and move south in December.

Other than Alaskan waters, they are not abundant anywhere in the Pacific. Frequently seen in Puget Sound and common along the central Californian coast in summer.

**Behavior:** Solitary or in twos and threes. Occasionally in large congregations. They often approach boats, particularly stationary vessels. Will enter shallow inshore waters.

They arch their tail when beginning a long dive but they do not raise their flukes clear of the water. They will breach by leaping clear of the water and reentering head first, smoothly. They will also occasionally splash like Humpbacks. They have been seen to spyhop in pack ice.

## FIELD MARKS:

medium, to 26 feet

sleek body

narrow, triangular head

white band on upper surface of
flippers

light chevron behind head

compare with Baird's Beaked
Whale and Northern
Bottlenose Whale

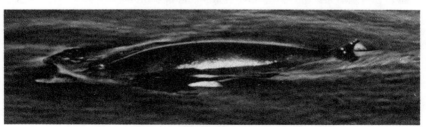

**Lookalikes:** Because of the setback of the dorsal fin, they can be confused with Baird's Beaked Whale or the Northern Bottlenose Whale, but both of those have bulbous heads and do not have a white stripe on their flipper. Can be distinguished from other rorquals by their much smaller size and white-banded flippers.

# NORTHERN BOTTLENOSE WHALE
*(Hyperoodon ampullatus)*

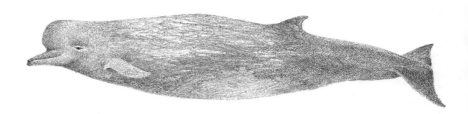

**Description:** Maximum length 32 feet. Dolphinlike, with a bulbous head and a long, distinct beak. Blow is upward or slightly forward; height to 6 feet, bushy, and can be seen from a considerable distance. Dorsal fin is erect, falcate, and located over two-thirds the way down the back. Flippers are short and tapered. Flukes have a very concave but unnotched trailing edge. Body color is usually dark brown, lighter on the sides. The belly may have patches of light gray. Very large animals, presumably older males, may have a white head. Body is often heavily scratched.

**Variability:** Young are uniform brown. Color and patterns change with age.

**Range:** In the western North Atlantic, they are found only in Arctic and north temperate water, generally offshore. They have been reported from Davis Straits to Narragansett Bay, Rhode Island. In spring and summer, they concentrate in the northern limits of their range, occasionally visiting the deep channels of the Gulf of St. Lawrence and eastern Newfoundland in summer.

**Behavior:** Often in groups up to 10 or more. Deep divers. They can stay submerged for well over one hour and rarely swim in waters shallower than 100 fathoms (600 feet). Low bushy blow. After a long dive, they may stay on the surface for 10 minutes or more, blowing regularly before rediving. They seldom raise their flukes before a long dive.

They have been seen to lobtail (raise their flukes and slap the water). They have also been seen to jump clear of the water. Often approach boats from a considerable distance.

**Lookalikes:** A first glance might confuse them with Minke Whale but the Minke Whale has a flat head, paired blowholes, and a white stripe on each flipper. Might also be confused with a Sperm Whale but the Sperm Whale has a more boxlike head, no dorsal fin, and notched flukes.

# KILLER WHALE
*(Orcinus orca)*

**Description:** Maximum length: 30 feet, male; 22 feet, female. Heavy, thick body. Body color is jet black with extensive areas of white from the jaw to the anal region. Oval white patch appears on the side of the head, above and behind the eyes. Tall, triangular-shaped dorsal fin in adult males. Large paddle-shaped flippers.

**Variability:** All black and all white specimens have been reported. Female dorsal fin often falcate and not as tall as adult male's.

**Range:** In Atlantic, from pack ice to Caribbean including Gulf of Mexico. Most common from New Jersey northward. Prefers coastal water. Arrives with the tuna, inshore in spring and summer. Migrates south as new ice forms. In the Pacific, common in and around Puget Sound, Vancouver Island, and the British Columbian and Alaskan coasts. Regularly sighted along the coast of California and near seal rookeries along Baja California.

**Behavior:** Very fast swimmers (to 25 knots). Travel in pods from a few to 30 individuals, occasionally herds of 100. Hunt cooperatively. Often breach and spyhop.

**Lookalikes:** Not likely to be confused with anything else if a male is present (with distinct dorsal fin) in the group. Females and immature animals can be confused with the False Killer Whale or Risso's Dolphin. False Killer Whale is shorter, more slender, and all black (some gray on belly), has a more tapered head, and thinner, longer flippers. Risso's Dolphin has a pothead, is heavily scarred, and does not have the large white patches of the Killer Whale.

## FIELD MARKS:

medium, to 30 feet

chunky

very tall, triangular dorsal fin

jet black body with white oval patches

# BELUGA OR WHITE WHALE

*(Delphinapterus leucas)*

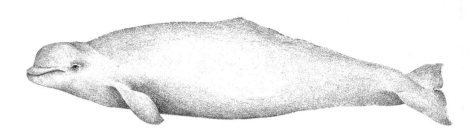

**Description:** Maximum length 16 feet. Robust, all-white body. No dorsal fin. At the mid-point of the back there is a narrow, bumpy ridge. The head is melon-shaped. Flippers are untapered. Body narrows considerably near the flukes.

**Variability:** Their young are an evenly colored brown that lightens to slate gray and then to white by their sixth or seventh year.

**Range:** In the Atlantic, from the Arctic Circle south as far as eastern Connecticut. Most abundant from the north shore of the Gulf of St. Lawrence northward. Regularly seen in the St. Lawrence and Saguenay Rivers through late spring and summer.

In the Pacific, they can be found in coastal waters adjacent to the Gulf of Alaska and farther north.

**Behavior:** Typically found in estuaries, although they range to oceanic waters. Often in large aggregations of more than 1,000 animals. Some animals have a seasonal north-south migration pattern while others stay in a specific area. They are at home in pack ice and can manage in places hostile to other whales and mammals. Often ascend far up rivers into fresh water. [Beluga Whales have been kept on live display for many years at the New York Zoological Society's Coney Island Aquarium.]

**Lookalikes:** Not likely to be confused with any other cetacean.

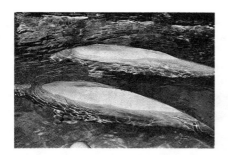

# FIELD MARKS:

medium, to 16 feet
.............
all white body
.............
melon-shaped head
.............
no dorsal fin
.............
cold water only
.............

# FALSE KILLER WHALE
*(Pseudorca crassidens)*

**Description:** Maximum length 18 feet. Body long and slender. Tapered head. Prominent creases on neck. Dorsal fin tall, falcate, with either a rounded or pointed peak.

Flippers situated well forward, long with a distinctive crook near the middle. Body color is all black, except for a blaze of gray on the belly between the flippers.

**Variability:** Head may be a lighter shade of black than the body. Shape of dorsal fin is variable.

**Range:** Widely distributed in warm, temperate, and tropical seas. Reported from Maryland south in the Atlantic to Gulf of Mexico and the Caribbean Sea. Rarely occurs in coastal waters, estuaries, or bays. In the Pacific, it is not abundant north of 30 degrees latitude. It has been sighted offshore of Washington, Oregon, and northern California, however. Large herds occasionally seen off Hawaii.

**Behavior:** Highly social, often in herds over 500. Herds of a dozen or so are more usual. Occasionally strands in great numbers. Will approach ships and bow ride. Will leap, slap down on their sides, and lobtail.

**Lookalikes:** Can be confused with immature and female Killer Whales that have a large distinct white oval patch on the side of their heads, and with Pilot Whales, whose heads are thick and bulbous and whose bodies are more robust. Can also be confused with the poorly known Pygmy Killer Whale and the Melon-head Whale, but is much larger than both (both average about 8 feet in length).

**FIELD MARKS:**

medium, to 18 feet

slender, all black body

falcate dorsal fin

gregarious

compare with Pilot Whale and
Risso's Dolphin

63

# ATLANTIC PILOT WHALE OR LONG-FINNED PILOT WHALE
## (*Globicephala melaena*)

**Description:** Maximum length: 20 feet, male; 18 feet, female. Head is bulbous and thick, particularly in males, hence the nickname pothead (as with the Short-finned Pilot Whale). Dorsal fin set well forward of the middle of the back. Dorsal fin has a long base and is usually rounded and falcate.

Body black on back and sides. Grayish white patch on chin and gray area on belly. Long flippers (to one-fifth of their body length), which are sickle-shaped.

**Variability:** Young animals are often light gray. Large, older whales often have a gray saddle behind their dorsal fin.

**Range:** Common off Labrador, Newfoundland, and in the St. Lawrence River. Sporadic south to Maryland and Virginia.

**Behavior:** Occurs in herds of up to 200 animals, although smaller groups (6 to 50) are more common. Sometimes associate with the Atlantic White-sided Dolphin. Often hang vertically in the water with their head and part of their back exposed. Often lobtail (raise their flukes and slap the water). Adults rarely breach, young do on occasion. Will not ride bow waves.

**Lookalikes:** Some range overlap with the Short-finned Pilot Whale and the False Killer Whale off Maryland and Virginia. The Long-finned Pilot has much longer flippers than the Short-finned Pilot Whale. The False Killer Whale has a more slender body and its dorsal fin, although falcate, is pointed at the tip. The False Killer Whale will ride bow waves and often "porpoise" and breach as it swims.

## FIELD MARKS:

medium, to 20 feet

bulbous forehead (pothead)

all black body

falcate dorsal fin

long flippers

compare with Short-finned Pilot Whale, False Killer Whale, and Risso's Dolphin

# SHORT-FINNED PILOT WHALE
*(Globicephala macrorhynchus)*

**Description:** Maximum length: 18 feet male; 13 feet, female. Thick, rounded, bulbous head, hence the nickname pothead. Robust body. Dorsal fin set well forward of the middle of the back, usually rounded and falcate. Body all black or dark brown except for a small patch of gray on the chin and belly. Flippers are long and sickle-shaped.

**Variability:** Some Pacific animals have a light gray saddle behind the dorsal fin and may also have a faint blaze between the blowhole and eye. Adult males are heavily scarred.

**Range:** In the Pacific, present but not common from Alaska to northern California. Abundant from Pt. Conception south. Common around Hawaii. In the Atlantic, they have been seen in Delaware Bay, but their normal range lies from Cape Hatteras (Virginia in summer) south to the Gulf of Mexico.

**Behavior:** Have been seen in groups of 60 or more but smaller groups are more common. Will mix with dolphins. Have been reported to skyhop and lobtail but rarely breach. They will occasionally bow ride.

**Lookalikes:** Can be confused with the Atlantic Pilot Whale, but its range is much farther south. In the tropics, it can be confused with the Pigmy Killer Whale and the Melon-headed Whale (neither covered here), but is larger than both (neither gets much longer than 8 feet) and has a much more distinctive dorsal fin. In the north Pacific, it can be confused with the False Killer Whale, which is rare above 30 degrees north latitude. Its head shape and dorsal fin will also distinguish the two. It has a more bulbous head and its dorsal fin is set much farther forward.

**FIELD MARKS:**

medium, to 18 feet
⋯⋯⋯⋯⋯
pothead
⋯⋯⋯⋯⋯
all black
⋯⋯⋯⋯⋯
falcate dorsal fin
⋯⋯⋯⋯⋯
compare with Atlantic Pilot
and False Killer Whales
⋯⋯⋯⋯⋯

# DOLPHINS
## (12 feet or less)

# RISSO'S DOLPHIN OR GRAMPUS
## *(Grampus griseus)*

**Description:** Maximum length 13 feet. Tubular body that narrows rapidly behind the dorsal fin. Somewhat bulbous head that is longitudinally divided by a V-shaped crease. No distinct beak. Tall, dark dorsal fin that is distinctly falcate. Flippers are long, curved, and pointed at tip. Body color is black above to grayish white on the chest and belly. Older adults often have large cream-white areas over body. All except young, which are uniformly gray, show heavy scratch marks or scars, and either white on black backgound or dark on light background.

**Variability:** Body color varies with age, as does degree of scarring.

**Range:** Temperate and tropical seas, generally oceanic, outside the 100 fathom line. Prefers warmer waters.

**Behavior:** Can be seen in herds of several hundred, although smaller groups of a dozen are much more common. Occasionally solitary. Often swims in chorus lines, evenly spaced in chevron formation. Often accompanies Pacific White-sided Dolphins, Northern Right Whale Dolphins, and Pilot Whales. Occasionally rides bow waves or stern wakes but normally ignores ships. Will porpoise when swimming and slap the water with its tail. It occasionally breaches.

**Lookalikes:** From a distance, they can be confused with the Bottlenose Dolphin. However, the presence of a beak in the Bottlenose and the scarring of the Grampus quickly separates them.

## FIELD MARKS:

medium, to 13 feet

blunt head

all black body, extensively scarred

falcate dorsal fin

gregarious, often swims in chorus lines

compare with False Killer Whale and Pilot Whale

# BOTTLENOSE DOLPHIN
*(Tursiops truncatus)*

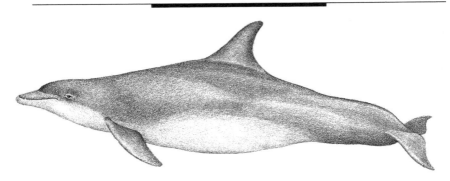

**Description:** Maximum length 12 feet. The well known Flipper of TV. Robust body, stubby snout, bulbous head, erect falcate dorsal fin. Color is silver to dark gray on its back, lighter on its sides, and pure white on its belly. The dark of the back often appears like a cape. Moderately sized flippers. Flukes are concave and separated by a notch.

**Variability:** Body color can vary from nearly black to silver gray.

**Range:** There is an oceanic and a coastal form in the Pacific. The same may be true for the Atlantic. Along Pacific shores it can be found from southern Los Angeles County south along Baja California to the Sea of Cortez. In the Atlantic, it is found offshore from Nova Scotia to North Carolina, and then both inshore and offshore to Florida, the Gulf of Mexico, and the Caribbean Sea.

**Behavior:** In the Atlantic, groups of a dozen or so often aggregate into large herds and frequently swim with the Atlantic Pilot Whale. They often accompany Right or Humpback Whales along the Atlantic side of the Florida coast. Small groups are common inshore. In the Pacific, large offshore herds swim with Pilot Whales, while others accompany migrating Gray Whales. In Hawaii in winter, they associate with Humpback Whales. They ride bow waves and are quite acrobatic—leaping, leap-frogging, and surf riding.

**Lookalikes:** Inshore, they can be confused with young Spotted Dolphins, which have a more slender head and whose color is more purple gray. Offshore, they can be confused with Risso's Dolphin at a distance and the Rough-toothed Dolphin. The shape of Risso's Dolphin and its heavy scarring soon separate it out. The Rough-toothed Dolphin has blotchy yellow spots on its skin and a more slender head and beak.

# COMMON DOLPHIN
*(Delphinus delphis)*

**Description:** Maximum length 8 feet. Long, well defined beak, usually black with a white tip. Tall dorsal fin can be falcate or nearly triangular. Back is black, the belly white, and the sides yellowish tan or gray. The black of the back forms a wide V or saddle under the dorsal fin. Up close, the pattern is a crisscross of tan, yellowish tan, and white.

**Variability:** Body color varies between black and brownish black. The colors below the saddle vary from tan to white.

**Range:** Widely distributed in temperate, subtropical, and tropical waters. Have been reported off Nova Scotia (summer and fall) south to the Caribbean and the Gulf of Mexico. In the Pacific, seldom north of Pt. Conception. Off southern California, peak abundance occurs in June, September through October, and January.

**Behavior:** Often associate with tuna. Can occur in herds of a thousand or more. Very active. When swimming they splash and jump frequently, often leaping clear of the water.

**Lookalikes:** Most easily confused with the Striped Dolphin because of the similarity of build and behavior. However, the Striped Dolphin is large, with two distinctive black stripes on each side that originate near the eye. The V-shaped saddle of the Common Dolphin will also help identify it.

## FIELD MARKS:

dolphinlike

to 8 feet

prominent beak

wide black V on sides

gregarious, in large herds

jump and splash frequently

compare with Striped Dolphin

# STRIPED DOLPHIN
### *(Stenella coeruleoalba)*

**Description:** Maximum length 9 feet. Body shape and size much like the Common Dolphin and Spotted Dolphin—slender, sleek, well defined beak, pointed flippers, and a falcate dorsal fin.

Their color pattern is distinctive, however. The top of the head and back is dark gray to bluish gray, sides are a lighter gray, the belly and throat are white. Belly is often bright pink. Dorsal fin, flippers, and flukes are dark. There are two black stripes on the lower half of each side—one from the eye to anus, the other from the eye to the flipper. The eye-to-flipper stripe is often double. The beak is black, and a black stripe extends from the beak to a black patch around the eye. A light shoulder blaze sweeps up from the underside forward of the dorsal fin. Another blaze often extends from underneath the midriff up and rearward toward the flukes.

**Variability:** Some contend that dolphins with a double stripe between the eye and the flipper constitute a separate species.

**Range:** Widely distributed in temperate, semitropical, and tropical seas. In the Atlantic, they have been reported from Nova Scotia to Jamaica. In the Pacific, mainly from 20 degrees latitude south. Common off Baja California.

**Behavior:** Gregarious, often in herds of several hundred. Will leap and splash when swimming. Will bow ride. Capable of amazing acrobatics—backward cartwheels, tailspins while airborne, and upside-down porpoising. Some associate with Yellowfin Tuna and are thus killed by purse seining.

**Lookalikes:** Can be confused with the Common Dolphin, but the lateral striping of the Striped Dolphin and the hourglass V-shape to the cape of the Common Dolphin easily separate the two.

## FIELD MARKS:

dolphinlike

to 9 feet

prominent beak

two black stripes on sides

compare with Common
Dolphin

# ATLANTIC WHITE-SIDED DOLPHIN
### (*Lagenorhynchus acutus*)

**Description:** Maximum length 9 feet. Robust body with a small beak. Dorsal fin is tall, highly falcate and pointed at its tip. Tail end of body does not taper until just before meeting the flukes. Curved flippers. The beak is black, the dorsal fin is gray or black, the back is black, the belly is white, and the sides have zones of gray, tan, and white. It has a distinct white oval patch along its side, from just beneath the dorsal fin rearward to an area just above the anus.

**Variability:** The fainter color patterns along its sides are variable.

**Range:** Primarily offshore in the cool waters between the Gulf Stream and the Labrador Current to as far south as Hudson Canyon.

**Behavior:** Can congregate in herds of a thousand, but smaller herds are more common. Wary of ships and will not bow ride. Often associated with the Atlantic Pilot Whale.

**Lookalikes:** Most likely to be confused with the White-beaked Dolphin. They look much alike, except for the oval patch along the sides of the White-sided Dolphin and its black beak.

dolphinlike

to 9 feet

long white patch on sides

dark beak usually

acrobatic

gregarious

compare with White-beaked
Dolphin

# PACIFIC WHITE-SIDED DOLPHIN
*(Lagenorhynchus obliquidens)*

**Description:** Maximum length 7 feet. Smoothly tapered head with a small beak. Dorsal fin is set in the middle of the back and is quite falcate, ending in a rounded tip. Flippers are curved with a concave trailing edge. Coloration is complex — the back is black, sides light gray, and belly white. Two white stripes run down the back like suspenders. The forward part of the dorsal fin is black and the remainder light gray. Most of the lower head is light gray, which extends back along the body well behind the flippers. Another light section occurs on the sides behind and below the dorsal fin and extends rearward to the flukes.

**Variability:** The size and coloration of the light gray areas of the sides vary among animals.

**Range:** As far north as the Aleutians and the Gulf of Alaska (summer), southward to the tip of Baja California. Often in large groups. Common around Cedros and Natividad Islands off Baja, and the Channel Islands off California, especially from October through February.

**Behavior:** Gregarious, in herds from 200 to several thousand. Often in the company of other dolphins and the California Sea Lion. Will approach close to shore if the water is deep. Will often run alongside a ship and will ride bow waves. Will jump clear of the water, often landing with a resounding smack. Occasionally, they will make complete somersaults.

**Lookalikes:** Can be confused from a distance with the Common Dolphin and Dall's Porpoise, but it has a much taller and more falcate dorsal fin than either, and is colored dark forward and lighter aft. Its two white body streaks (suspenders) are quite distinctive.

# WHITE-BEAKED DOLPHIN
## (*Lagenorhynchus albirostris*)

**Description:** Maximum length 10 feet. Robust body. Short, thick beak that is colored white or light gray. Dark gray body with white or light gray body. Two light pale areas on sides—one in front of and below the dorsal fin, the other behind it. Dorsal fin moderately falcate and always dark.

**Variability:** Beaks of western North Atlantic dolphins less frequently white than eastern Atlantic relatives.

**Range:** From Cape Cod north to Greenland, Newfoundland, Labrador, and Davis Strait. Common off Newfoundland and Labrador in summer and autumn. Migrates southward to Cape Cod in winter and is common thereabouts from April to June.

**Behavior:** Occasionally seen in large herds (to 1000 animals), but along the North American coast small pods of 25 or less more common. Can be acrobatic. Seldom seen around ships.

**Lookalikes:** Can be confused with the Atlantic White-sided Dolphin but its dorsal fin is more prominent, and it has pale sides and often a white beak.

**FIELD MARKS:**

dolphinlike
..............
to 10 feet
..............
dark, falcate dorsal fin
..............
white beak, usually
..............
light areas on sides
..............
gregarious
..............
compare with White-sided
Dolphin
..............

The White-beaked Dolphin is not at all easy to distinguish from the White-sided Dolphin in the water except if it has a white beak. A stranded specimen will show the lack of the prominent, elongated white patch seen in the White-sided Dolphin.

# SPOTTED DOLPHIN
*(Stenella plagiodon)(Atlantic)*
*(Stenella attenuata)(Pacific)*

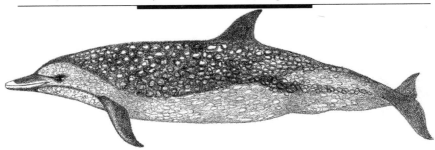

**Description:** Maximum length 8 feet. Unspotted when young, light or dark spots begin to appear when animal is 4 1/2 feet long and is heavily spotted by adulthood. Their adult shape is much like a Bottlenose Dolphin. *S. plagiodon* has a falcate dorsal fin, a slender head, and a long beak whose lips and snout tip are often white. *S. attenuata* contains several races — a coastal species off Mexico that is heavily spotted, and a Hawaiian race that is hardly spotted at all.

**Variability:** Mainly the degree of spotting that increases with age (except for the Hawaiian race, which can be quickly identified by its distinct white lips and snout).

**Range:** A tropical species in the Pacific. The northern coastal race does not occur north of the United States–Mexican border. In the Atlantic, they have been said to have been seen as far north as New Jersey, but are most common from Cape Hatteras south into the Caribbean and the Gulf of Mexico. The Gulf population has been known to approach the shore in spring and summer. Normally, they keep more than 5 miles offshore but within the 100 fathom line.

**Behavior:** Can occur in herds of several hundred, but small groups much more common. They leap clear of the water while swimming and will ride bow waves. They can be seen at long distances because of the froth they create while swimming. In the Pacific, aggregations often exceed 1,000 animals and can be mixed with Spinner Dolphins. They and the Spinner Dolphin associate with tuna and have suffered heavy losses from purse seining. Many no longer ride bow waves but flee from the sound of boat engines.

**Lookalikes:** Offshore, Pacific Spotted Dolphin can be distinguished from Spinner Dolphins by their falcate dorsal fin (Spinners have a triangular fin). Young Spotted Dolphins are very hard to separate from Bottlenose Dolphins, but are invariably accompanied by adults.

## FIELD MARKS:

dolphinlike

to 8 feet

heavily spotted, light on dark

falcate dorsal fin

create much froth when
swimming

acrobatic

compare with Spinner Dolphin

# SPINNER DOLPHIN
*(Stenella longirostris)*

**Description:** Maximum length 7 feet. Slender body, slender beak that is dark on top and white below (on some white may show on top). Tip of snout distinctly black. Back is dark gray to black, sides tan or yellowish brown, belly white. Erect dorsal fin triangular to moderately falcate.

**Variability:** Beak may be extremely long. Body color of large animals may be almost all black with light speckling. Exhibits worldwide race differences (the short-beaked form is thought by some to be a separate species).

**Range:** Oceanic and tropical seas. Occur off Florida, Gulf of Mexico, West Indies, western tropical Pacific, and Hawaiian Islands.

**Behavior:** Often in large herds mixed with Spotted Dolphins. While swimming, they leap clear of the water with considerable splashing. Frequently ride bow waves; however, in the Pacific, where many have been lost to tuna boat seiners, they now run from motorized ships. Often leap high out of the water and somersault end-over-end (hence the name spinner).

**Lookalikes:** Their erect dorsal fin, long beak, and leaping activity distinguishes them from other dolphins of the same size.

**FIELD MARKS:**

dolphinlike

to 7 feet

long beak

erect dorsal fin

acrobatic, often somersault

often with Spotted Dolphin

# NORTHERN RIGHT WHALE DOLPHIN
## (*Lissodelphis borealis*)

**Description:** Maximum length: 9 feet, male; 7 feet, female. Long, slender body tapering to a narrow tail stock and flukes. Flukes sharply pointed. Body looks almost eellike — no forehead, chin, dorsal fin, or dorsal ridges.

Body is black except for the white belly. White area is broad in front of the flippers and narrows from the flippers to the tail stock. Tip of jaw may be white. Flukes are light gray above and off-white below.

**Variability:** Overall body color can be brownish rather than black. The white pattern underneath can vary with sex and among individuals. Young are much lighter in color — cream to light gray.

**Range:** Eastern North Pacific, in temperate waters between 30° north and 50° north latitude. Will move farther south if water temperatures are unseasonably low. Usually present year round off central and northern California just off the continental shelf, and are relatively abundant from Point Sur to Pt. Conception and the Channel Islands. Less common off Oregon, Washington, and British Columbia.

**Behavior:** Gregarious, often in herds of 100 or more. Often seen with the Pacific White-sided Dolphin. Fast swimmers, up to 18 knots. They run from approaching vessels, either by swimming just below the surface or by making low leaps.

When swimming, all tend to be airborne simultaneously, but they leap on an even keel, unlike the Pacific White-sided Dolphin. They occasionally belly flop, side slap, and lobtail. Occasionally ride bow waves. Usually found in the company of Pacific White-sided Dolphins.

**Lookalikes:** At slow speed or when leaping low rapidly, they look like sea lions or fur seals.

# FIELD MARKS:

sleek body

to 9 feet

no dorsal fin

black with white belly, white
patch behind flippers

white lips

can be mistaken for a fur seal
or sea lion

Northern Right Whale Dolphins are wary of boats and when running from them, can work the sea to quite a froth.

# PORPOISES
## (less than 7 feet)

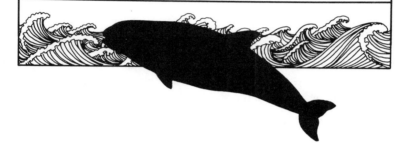

# DALL'S PORPOISE
*(Phocoenoides dalli)*

**Description:** Maximum length 7 feet. Stocky, so much so that the head and flukes look disproportionately small. Steep forehead, poorly defined beak. Dorsal fin is triangular to moderately falcate with a long base. Flippers are small, located far forward on the body. Tail section has a pronounced keel. Striking black-and-white color pattern. Animal is basically shiny black with a large, conspicuous white patch on each side from the midriff aft. The upper half of the dorsal fin is white, as is the trailing edge of the flukes.

**Variability:** Mainly in color—body may be gray or brownish black; white areas may be speckled.

**Range:** Most common small cetacean in the North Pacific. Abundant in Alaskan waters (year round in Prince William Sound and Glacier Bay), inshore waters of British Columbia and Washington, and as far south as California's Channel Islands, where it usually remains offshore outside the 100-fathom line. In winter and spring it swims south and more inshore along the California and Baja California coasts.

**Behavior:** Usually swims in bands of 2 to 20. Often in mixed herds with the Pacific White-sided Dolphin. Will bow ride. Extremely fast swimmer and will throw up enough wake and spray to obscure a view of it. They almost never leap clear of the water.

**Lookalikes:** Not likely to be confused with any other cetacean.

## FIELD MARKS:

stocky
...............

to 7 feet
...............

large white patch on side
...............

white on dorsal fin and flukes
...............

Dall's Porpoise splashes so much that you may not get a clear look until it bowrides the boat. Then, by its size and coloration, it is unmistakable.

# HARBOR PORPOISE
*(Phococena phocoena)*

**Description:** Maximum length 5 feet. Small chunky body colored gray or brown on the back, fading to light gray or brown on the sides. White belly. White extends up the sides in front of the flippers, which can be seen when the animal leaps. No snout or prominent forehead. Triangular dorsal fin. Trailing edges of flukes are concave and divided by a distinct notch.

**Variability:** Mainly in body color—sides often speckled with white. Occasional albinos have been seen.

**Range:** Common in northern bays, harbors, river mouths, and shallow inshore waters. In the Atlantic, common from Labrador to Massachusetts. In the Pacific, common to sporadic from southeast Alaska to northern California.

**Behavior:** Occasionally seen in large aggregations, but more often singly, paired, or in small groups of 5 to 10 individuals. Rarely associates with dolphins, but sometimes seen with Fin and Humpback Whales along the Canadian coast in summer. Rarely breaches, but does leap and splash the surface when swimming fast. Will not approach boats or bow ride.

**Lookalikes:** Not likely to be confused with any other cetacean.

## FIELD MARKS:

chunky

small, to 4 feet

white patch on sides

flukes notched

travel in small groups

95

# APPENDIXES

# APPENDIX 1

## Where To See Whales

Off the United States coastline, some species of whales and dolphins pass by close to shore on their way to feeding or breeding grounds. Other species keep well offshore, so the best chance of seeing them is from an ocean-going vessel. Some species deliberately avoid boats and shorelines (Beaked Whales, for example) so they are seldom sighted. Other species are seldom seen because there are so few of them. Some whales are difficult to distinguish from more common species (Sei Whales, for instance, are not easy to separate from lookalikes).

There are, however, hot spots for some species of whales where, in certain months of the year, sightings can be almost guaranteed. To the north, these are mainly feeding areas, to the south, breeding and calving grounds. Although the same individuals and families often return to the same feeding grounds year after year, check with local authorities on whether the whales are present. A sudden drop in the population of fish can send them elsewhere, as fast as you would change supermarkets if you found the shelves empty in your usual store.

Information on where to write or call is listed at the end of this appendix.

### Northeast

Newfoundland and Labrador waters offer good whalewatching, but traveling there requires advanced planning. Along the St. Lawrence River in summer and early fall, especially near the mouth of the Saguenay River near Grandes-Bergeronnes, Quebec, you can see Blue and Beluga Whales from shore. You can also spot whales from the various ferries across the St. Lawrence between its north and south shores or from local whalewatch boats. Lists of sightings include the Blue Whale, Beluga, Fin, Minke, Humpback, Killer Whale, Atlantic Pilot Whale, Atlantic White-sided Dolphin, White-beaked Dolphin, and Harbor Porpoise. Write Tourisme-Quebec for more details. Be sure to ask specifically for a tourist guide to Manicouagan. It lists full particulars on a number of relatively inexpensive whalewatch boats from a series of locations near the confluence of the St. Lawrence and Saguenay Rivers.

At the mouth of the Bay of Fundy, either from New Brunswick or Nova Scotia, you can see the Right Whale, Humpback, Fin, Minke, Atlantic White-sided Dolphin, Harbor Porpoise, and perhaps a Blue Whale, Sei, Beluga, Killer Whale, or White-beaked Dolphin.

In New Brunswick, there are good observation points on Grand Manan Island, which can be reached by ferry. Deer Island and Campobello Island also offer shore sighting possibilities. Write Tourism New Brunswick.

In Nova Scotia, the best viewing areas from land are on Brier Island and Digby

Neck. Many other shore locations, as well as boat trips, are available well north to Cape Breton Island. The ferries that connect Nova Scotia and New Brunswick can also serve as whalewatching trips. Write Nova Scotia Tourism.

In northern Maine, you can see Fin, Humpback, Minke, and Right Whales from shore in Quoddy Head State Park in late summer. Whalewatching boat trips leave from Lubec, Bar Harbor, Rockland, Portland, and other cities in summer. Write the Maine Publicity Bureau.

Off New Hampshire and Massachusetts, Humpback, Fin, and Minke Whales are relatively common. You may also sight the Right Whale, the Atlantic Pilot Whale, and an occasional Sei, Beluga, Killer, or Sperm Whale, as well as Risso's Dolphin, the Atlantic White-sided Dolphin, and the Bottlenose Dolphin. During June to September, whalewatch boats leave from Portsmouth and Newburyport, New Hampshire, Gloucester, Boston, Plymouth, and Provincetown, Massachusetts. Provincetown is by far the whalewatching capital of the eastern seaboard, because it is such a short trip to Stellwagen Bank and whale sightings are almost guaranteed. You can make arrangements in advance, or just show up at MacMillian Pier and take the next available boat.

## Middle Atlantic

Whalewatching boats leave regularly from Montauk, Long Island, with variable success. Other charters requiring advanced booking run to offshore canyons occasionally from ports in southern New Jersey and from Ocean City, Maryland. Whales are often sighted along the edge of the continental shelf, but it's a long trip and the whales are not always there when you arrive. Along the middle Atlantic, you may occasionally see Bottlenose Dolphins inshore as well as the occasional stray whale. A solitary whale may often stay in a particular area for a few days, and local fishermen will be aware of its presence.

## Southeast and Gulf

Inshore, especially in winter, Bottlenose Dolphins are common. Now and then, you may also see a Spotted Dolphin or a Short-finned Pilot Whale. At Indian River, Florida, not only are Bottlenose Dolphins likely, but also the West Indian Manatee. The Manatee is also common in winter in Crystal River, Florida. Sightings along the Florida coast and in the Gulf are too uncertain to support a whalewatching tour boat trade.

## Pacific Northwest

Off southern Alaskan waters, the Gray Whale, Humpback, Beluga, Killer Whale, and Fin Whale are common in summer. So is Dall's Porpoise. You may also occasionally see a Sperm, Blue, or Sei Whale, as well as the Pacific White-sided Dolphin. The Right Whale, Baird's Beaked Whale, and the Northern

Bottlenose Whale have been sighted on rare occasions. Although there are many good lookouts from land off south central Alaska (Kodiak Island is one of them) and among the straits and inlets of the southeastern Alaskan coast, especially between Juneau and Prince Rupert, getting there almost always requires a boat trip. Your best bet is the State of Alaska ferry service, which runs as far south as Seattle. Write the Alaska Marine Highway for schedules.

In March and April, the western shore of Vancouver Island has a number of vantage points from which you can see migrating Gray Whales, as well as Killer Whales, and Dall's Porpoise. You may also occasionally see a Minke, Humpback, Blue, Sei, Sperm Whale, and the Pacific White-sided Dolphin. Killer Whales are common in the straits between Vancouver Island and the mainland. Boat tours are available out of Vancouver. Write Tourism BC. Ask for the latest update of the "Whalewatching and Marine Wildlife Tours" brochure. It covers cruise information, land lookouts, guidelines for approaching whales with your own boat, information on festivals, oceanaria, and more.

## Washington, Oregon, Northern and Central California

One of the best places to see Killer Whales is the San Juan Islands, particularly between June and September. There is a whale museum at Friday Harbor that keeps track of local sightings. For ferry schedules and other whalewatch boats, write Washington State Department of Commerce and General Development. They will also send you information on charters, rentals, and a travel guide to the San Juan Islands.

Almost any promontory along the outer coast of Washington, Oregon, and northern and central California will do to see migrating Gray Whales; southward from October to December, and northward from March to May. A great number of boats take out tourists. Almost every harbor of consequence has someone in the business during the migration season.

Whalewatch charters can be arranged from Neah Bay and Westport, Washington, and Garabaldi, Tillamook, and Charleston, Oregon.

In California, tour boats leave from Crescent City, Eureka, Fort Bragg, Santa Cruz, Monterey, and Morro Bay, among other places. Trips from San Francisco can be arranged to the Farallone Islands, where a number of species can be sighted aside from Gray Whales. For a list of tours, write the California Office of Tourism. Their brochure also includes information about watching migrating Gray Whales from state parks.

### Southern California to the Sea of Cortez

Shore sites for viewing passing Gray Whales are plentiful in California and along the Baja Peninsula. Daily whalewatch trips leave from Santa Barbara, Ventura, the seaside towns around Los Angeles, Newport Beach, Dana Point, and San Diego. San Diego is the jumping off point for multi-day whalewatch trips to the Channel Islands and, from January to mid-March, tours to Baja California and the mouth of the Sea of Cortez. Information on these longer expeditions can be obtained directly from tour operators. Check the classified section of *Natural History* magazine for their ads.

The *New York Times* Sunday travel section usually runs a fall feature on west coast whalewatching. Ask them for the publication date of its next appearance. It lists a great many sites and boats for the entire coast.

### Hawaii

If you want to see Spinner and Spotted Dolphins, as well as Humpback and False Killer Whales, the west side of Maui is a good place to look. Numerous boat tours leave from Lahaina in west Maui. For more information, write Hawaii Visitor's Bureau. Unfortunately, their brochures barely mention whalewatching.

## *Keeping A Log*

If you become a dedicated whalewatcher, keeping a log will not only provide you with useful information as the years pass, but can be extremely helpful to institutions that study the life histories of whales.

To record a sighting, your first problem is identification. Train yourself to ask the following questions.

- How large is the animal?
- Does it have a dorsal fin or dorsal hump? If so, what is the size, shape, and position of the fin or hump?
- Did you see the animal blow? If so, how high, what shape and how frequently?
- What color and what color patterns could you see?
- Does the animal have any distinctive markings?
- Did it show its tail flukes? Can you describe their shape?
- Did it approach, avoid, or ignore the vessel? Did it ride the bow wave or stern wake?

- How does the animal behave? Does it leap from the water? What sort of acrobatics does it do?
- How long was it on the surface between dives? What was its dive interval?
- Are any of the animals tagged? If so, what is their size, shape, color, and position on the animal's body? Can you read a number or symbol?

The more you can glean while actually observing the animal, the more likely you can make a positive identification. Don't be dismayed if you cannot positively identify your sighting. Many a cetologist has the same difficulty in certain sea conditions and with certain species.

If you can take photographs, do so. You will usually need a telephoto lens. Use the longest focal length you can and still get a sharp image. Photos of flukes and dorsal fins that show specific markings can be useful in tracking specific individuals.

If you don't have or use a camera, a sketch can be helpful. Make special note of the positions of scratches or odd markings. These often can be used to identify a specific animal.

After you gather your sighting information, ask the boat captain for your position. LORAN numbers will do as well as latitude and longitude. If neither is available, make a best estimate of your position from time, speed, and compass direction (e.g. 4 hours at 12 knots, due west of Barnegat Inlet. If near shore, land bearings can be helpful.

A typical SIGHTING INFORMATION LOG follows. One is filled out to give you an idea of what you might record, the other is blank so that you may make mechanical copies for your own log.

If you come across a stranded animal, notify any nearby institution (see Appendix 3), and they will send someone to take appropriate measurements and perhaps perform an autopsy. If the animal or animals are alive, contact local authorities immediately. Occasionally, these animals can either be persuaded to return to sea or taken to facilities and nursed back to health.

## SIGHTING INFORMATION LOG

DATE, TIME _July 9, 1992  2 PM_ POSITION _Stellwagen Bank; about 1 hr at 12 knots due EAST of Provincetown, MA._

WEATHER CONDITIONS _Sunny, about 75° F, visibility 6 miles, winds calm_

SEA CONDITIONS _1-3 ft. sea. No whitecaps_

---

SPECIES _Humpback Whales (Megaptera Noveangliae) All adult size_

NUMBER ___6___ HEADING _milling_ SPEED _____

OTHER ANIMALS _1 Fin Whale (Balaenoptera Physalus)_
_Few herring gulls nearby_

---

UNUSUAL MARKINGS; TAGS _Got pix of two tail flukes._
_A third whale had a chunk of left flipper missing (see sketch)_

---

BASIS OF IDENTIFICATION. _Knobbed head, arched dive, hooked dorsal fin, ragged flippers, size over 40 feet, flukes exposed during dive_

BEHAVIOR _Dived repeatedly; several allowed ship to approach One raised and slapped flipper (piece missing)_

SKETCHES

|← ———— 30-40ft ————— →|

piece missing

Fin Whale (?)   500 yds away
flukes didn't surface when it dived.

---

PHOTOS? _Yes_ PHOTO REFERENCE ___W 7-9-92___

ADDITONAL REMARKS _Whales repeatedly dived (apparently feeding) but never became acrobatically active. Saw fin once. It dove and vanished._

---

NAME AND ADDRESS OF SHIP AND OBSERVER _Dolphin III whalewatch boat Macmillan Pier Provincetown. Observed by Tom Richard 123 Water Street, Fairwood N.J. 07733_

## SIGHTING INFORMATION LOG

DATE, TIME _____ POSITION _____

WEATHER CONDITIONS _____
SEA CONDITIONS _____

SPECIES _____
NUMBER _____ HEADING _____SPEED _____
OTHER ANIMALS _____

UNUSUAL MARKINGS; TAGS _____

BASIS OF IDENTIFICATION. _____

BEHAVIOR _____

SKETCHES

PHOTOS? _____ PHOTO REFERENCE _____
ADDITONAL REMARKS _____

NAME AND ADDRESS OF SHIP AND OBSERVER _____

# Information on Local Whalewatching Activities

The following organizations and agencies can be contacted for information on whalewatching in specific areas.

## Eastern Canada

Nova Scotia Tourism
Box 456
Halifax, Nova Scotia
B3J2R5 Canada
(800) 341-6096

Tourism Newfoundland
Box 2016
St John's, Newfoundland
A1C5R8 Canada
(800) 563-6353

Tourisme Quebec
CP20 000
Quebec City, Quebec
G1K7X2 Canada
(800) 443-7000

Tourism New Brunswick
Box 12345
Fredericton, New Brunswick
E3B 5C3 Canada
(800) 561-0123

## Northeastern United States

Maine Publicity Bureau
97 Winthrop Street
Hallowell, ME 04347
(207) 289-2423

Massachusetts Office of Travel and Tourism
100 Cambridge Street, 13th Floor
Boston, MA 02202
(800) 447-MASS

New Hampshire Office of Vacation Travel
Box 856
Concord, NH 03301
(603) 271-2666

## Pacific Coast

Alaska State Division of Tourism
E-28
Juneau, AK 99801
(907) 465-2010

Alaska Marine Highway
Box 25535R
Juneau, AK 99802
(800) 642-0066

California Office of Tourism
1121 L Street, Suite 103
Sacramento, CA 95814
(800) TO-CALIF

Delagacion Federal
Plaza de la Constitucion
Entre Belisario Dominguezy 5 de Mayo
La Paz, B. C., Mexico

Department of Trade and Economic Development
101 General Administration Building, AX-13
Olympia, WA 98504
(206) 753-5600

Economic Development Department
595 Cottage Street, NE
Salem, OR 97310
(800) 547-7842

Hawaii Visitors Bureau
2270 Kalakaua Avenue, Suite 801
Honolulu, HI 96813
(808) 923-1811

San Diego Convention and Visitors Bureau
1200 3rd Avenue, Suite 824
San Diego, CA 92101
(619) 232-3101
Most whale trips to Mexican waters originate in San Diego

State Secretary of Tourism of Baja California
Box 2448
Chula Vista, CA 92012
(706) 684-2126

Tourism British Columbia
Parliament Buildings
Victoria, BC
V8W2Z2 Canada

Whales and Friends
550 2nd Street
Oakland, CA 94607
(510) 763-0585

# APPENDIX 2

*Species List of Whales, Dolphins, and Porpoises of the Western North Atlantic and the Eastern North Pacific Waters*

| Common Name | Scientific Name | Occurrence** |
| --- | --- | --- |
| *Baleen Whales* | *Suborder Mysticeti* | |
| | | |
| **Rorquals** | Family Balaenopteridae | |
| * Blue | Balaenoptera musculus | A–P** |
| * Fin | Balaenoptera physalus | A–P |
| * Sei | Balaenoptera borealis | A–P |
| * Bryde's | Balaenoptera edeni | A–P |
| * Humpback | Megaptera novaeangliae | A–P |
| * Minke | Balaenoptera acutorostrata | A–P |
| **Right Whales** | Family Balaenidae | |
| Bowhead | Balaena mysticetus | A–P |
| * Right | Eubalaena glacialis | A–P |
| **Gray Whales** | Family Eschrichtidae | |
| * Gray | Eschrichtius robustus | P |
| | | |
| *Toothed Whales* | *Suborder Odontoceni* | |
| | | |
| **Beaked Whales** | Family Ziphiidae | |
| North Sea BWh | Mesoplodon bidens | A |
| Hubb's BWh | Mesoplodon carlhubbsi | P |
| Blainville's BWh | Mesoplodon densirostris | A–P |
| Antillean BWh | Mesoplodon europaeus | A |
| Ginkgo-toothed BWh | Mesoplodon ginkgodens | P |
| Hector's BWh | Mesoplodon hectori | P |
| True's BWh | Mesoplodon mirus | A |
| Stejneger's BWh | Mesoplodon stejnegeri | P |
| Cuvier's BWh | Ziphius cavirostris | A–P |
| (Goosebeaked whale) | | |
| Southern Bottlenose | Hyperoodon sp. | P |
| * Northern Bottlenose | Hyperoodon ampullatus | A |
| * Baird's BWh | Berardius bairdii | P |

| Sperm Whales | Family Physeteridae | |
| --- | --- | --- |
| * Sperm | Physeter macrocephalus (catodon) | A–P |
| Pygmy Sperm | Kogia breviceps | A–P |
| Dwarf Sperm | Kogia simus | A–P |
| **Monodonts** | Family Monodontidae | |
| Narwhal | Monodon monoceros | A–P |
| * Beluga (White) | Delphinapterus leucas | A–P |
| **Dolphins** | Family Delphinidae | |
| Rough-toothed Dolphin | Steno bredanensis | A–P |
| Melon-headed Whale | Peponocephala electra | A–P |
| Pygmy Killer Whale | Feresa attenuata | A–P |
| * Killer Whale | Orcinus orca | A–P |
| * False Killer Whale | Pseudorca crassidens | A–P |
| * Atlantic Pilot Whale | Globicephala melaena | A |
| * Short-finned Pilot Whale | Globicephala macrorhynchus | A–P |
| * Risso's Dolphin (Grampus) | Grampus griseus | A–P |
| * Bottlenose Dolphin | Tursiops truncatus | A–P |
| * Common Dolphin (Saddleback Dolphin) | Delphinus delphis | A–P |
| * Striped Dolphin | Stenella coeruleoalba | A–P |
| * Atlantic White-sided Dolphin | Lagenorhynchus acutus | A |
| * Pacific White-sided Dolphin | Lagenorhynchus obliquidens | P |
| * White-beaked Dolphin | Lagenorhynchus albirostris | A |
| Fraser's Dolphin | Lagenodelphis hosei | A–P |
| * Spotted Dolphin | Stenella attenuata | P |
| * Spotted Dolphin | Stenella plagiodon | A |
| Bridled Dolphin | Stenella frontalis | A |
| * Spinner Dolphin | Stenella longirostris | A–P |
| * Northern Right Whale Dolphin | Lissodelphis borealis | P |
| **Porpoises** | Family Phocoenidae | |
| * Dall's Porpoise | Phocoenoides dalli | P |
| * Harbor Porpoise | Phocoena phocoena | A–P |
| Cochito | Phocoena sinus | P |

*   Specific information on these entries is found in this book.
** A–Atlantic Ocean
    P–Pacific Ocean

# APPENDIX 3

## *Institutions that have Scientific Concerns About Whales*

(Also see references in Corrigan (1991), Hoyt (1984), and Pacheco and Smith (1989).

Allied Whale
College of the Atlantic
Bar Harbor, ME 04609
(207) 288-5644

American Cetacean Society
P.O. Box 2639
San Pedro, CA 90737

Brier Island Ocean Study
Westport, Nova Scotia
B0V 1H0 Canada

Cabrillo Marine Museum
3720 Stephen White Drive
San Pedro,CA 90731
(213) 548-7562

California Marine Mammal Center
Marin Headlands Ranger Station
Fort Cronkhite, CA 94965

Center for Coastal Studies
59 Commercial Street, Box 1036
Provincetown, MA 02657
(617) 487-3622

Center for Whale Research
1359 Smugglers Cove
Friday Harbor, WA 98250

Cetacean Research Unit
P.O. Box 159
Gloucester, MA 01930

Cetacean Society International
P.O. Box 9145
Wethersfield, CT 06109

Interpretative Center of Mileau Marin
102 Rue de la Cale-seche
Tadoussac, Quebec
G0T 2A0 Canada
(418) 235-4646

Marine Mammal Stranding Center
3625 Brigantine Blvd, PO Box 773
Brigantine NJ 08203
(609) 266-0538

Mingan Island Cetacean Study
*summer:*
P.O. Box 159
Sept-Iles, Quebec
G4R 4K3 Canada

*winter:*
285 rue Green
St. Lambert, Quebec
J4P 1T3 Canada

Mote Marine Laboratory
1600 Thompson Parkway
City Island
Sarasota, Fl 34236
(813) 388-4441

Newfoundland Museum
285 Duckworth Street
St. Johns, Newfoundland
A1C 1G9 Canada
(709) 737-2460

Nova Scotia Museum
1747 Summer Street
Halifax, Nova Scotia
B3H 3A6 Canada
(902) 429-4610

Ocean Research and
Education Society, Inc.
19 Harbor Loop
Gloucester, MA 01930
(617) 283-1475

Ocean Sciences Center
Memorial University of Newfoundland
St. Johns, Newfoundland
A1C 5S7 Canada
(709) 726-4888

Okeanos Ocean Research Foundation
Box 776
Hampton Bays, NY 11946

Pacific Whale Foundation
Kealia Beach Plaza Suite 21
101 North Kihei Road
Kihei, Maui, HI 96753

San Diego Natural History Museum
El Prado in Balboa Park
Box 1390
San Diego, CA 92112
(619) 232-7562

Société Lineené Saint-Laurent
CP 9880 Sle-Foy, Quebec
GIV 4C5 Canada
(418) 653-8186

Steinhart Aquarium
California Academy of Sciences
Golden Gate Park
San Francisco, CA 94118
(415) 221-5100

University of British Columbia
Centre for Continuing Education
5997 Iona Drive, Vancouver, BC
V6T2A4 Canada
(604) 228-2181

Whale Study Center
Mystic Marine Aquarium
Mystic, CT 06355

# SELECTED BIBLIOGRAPHY

Bennett, B. 1983. *The Oceanic Society Field Guide to the Gray Whale*. Legacy Publishing Co., San Francisco. 51 pp.

Bulloch, D. 1991. *The Underwater Naturalist*. Lyons & Burford, New York. 276 pp.

Corrigan, P. 1991. *Where the Whales Are*. Globe Pequot Press, Chester, CT. 326 pp.

Ellis, R. 1980. *The Book of Whales*. Alfred A. Knopf, New York 252 pp.

Ellis, R. 1982. *Dolphins and Porpoises*. Alfred A. Knopf, New York. 248 pp.

Hardy, A. 1967. *Great Waters*. Harper and Row, New York. 542 pp.

Heintzelman, D. 1981. *A World Guide to Whales, Dolphins, and Porpoises*. Winchester Press, Tulsa, OK. 156 pp.

Hoyt, E. 1984. *The Whale Watcher's Handbook*. Doubleday & Co., New York. 208 pp.

Katona, S., et. al. 1975. *A Field Guide to the Whales and Seals of the Gulf of Maine*. Maine Coastal Press, Rochester, ME. 97 pp.

Leatherwood, S., R. Reeves, and L. Foster. 1983. *The Sierra Club Handbook of Whales and Dolphins*. Sierra Club Books, San Francisco. 302 pp.

Lyall, S. 1981. *Sea Guide to Whales of the World*. Elsevier-Dutton Publishing Co., NY. 302 pp.

Matthews, L.H. 1968. *The Natural History of the Whale*. Columbia University Press, New York. 219 pp.

Norris, K.N. 1991. *Dolphin Days: The Life and Times of the Spinner Dolphin*. W.W. Norton Co., New York. 335 pp.

Pacheco, A. and S. Smith 1989. *Marine Parks and Aquaria*. Lyons & Burford, New York. 164 pp.

Scheffer, V.B. 1969. *The Year of the Whale*. Charles Scribner's Sons, New York. 213 pp.

Slijper, E.J. 1979. *Whales*. Cornell University Press, Ithaca, New York. 511 pp.

# INDEX

# INDEX